novum pocket

Goreti Marinho

Poems by
Heart

novum pocket

© 2024 novum publishing

ISBN 978-3-903468-66-5
Editing: Vaughn Chambers
Cover photo & Internal illustrations:
Maria Marinho
Cover design, layout & typesetting:
novum publishing

The images provided by the author
have been printed in the highest
possible quality.

www.novum-publishing.co.uk

Print product with financial
climate contribution
ClimatePartner.com/16547-2311-1001

Contents

1 – One man and his orchestra

Make the people of the world enjoy music,
smiles, love, and freedom.
Our hearts are full of love
To share
With our families, friends,
and the ones in despair.
Moments of happiness
Don't last long
But keep us happy and strong.
Don't give up on a bad day
Tomorrow will be better anyway.
Hope is here to last.
Sometimes things go too fast,
Hope is here to stay,
Strength, attitude, love, and trust.
All the benisons from above,
The bad things will pass.
Beautiful thoughts may last.

2 – We are all one

Colour,
Why say,
I'm black or white?
Equality is our biggest right.
Look at a human's heart,
Beautiful no doubt.
People of the world,
You are blessed by nature,
and the lord.
Colour is not just to differentiate,
But to treat everything and everyone with
Love and respect.
Colourful or not we must appreciate
Everyone as a soulmate.

3 – In the park

Here again
With sunshine making all the leaves
Shadows on the path,
Wind's gentle blow feeling kindle touched.
Colourful is looking up,
Green looking down
It's the bush and the grass.
The tree arms hugging other trees,
Roots firm showing on the ground.
Stay firm
Even if you feel down.
Wondering what was next,
The ducklings following their mother
Trying their best.
Feel warm, skin is free
Light as it can be.
My eyes see the wonders of our world.
Thank you is my word.
I am here, in this lovely space,
It's real, I'm glad it's not fake.
Peaceful in my heart;
Thoughts of compassion
And kindness
I remember, I brought them to myself.
I want to say
You brought the best in me
Today.

4 – The Gift

I met you,
Just smile;
Told you a poem
You were impressed for a while.
I don't know what to say,
But I believe God is guiding me all the way.
All I want is to bring a smile,
Forget things can be hard for a while.
I have no tears but I have some fears.
I'm giving gratitude, kindness, and love
All free,
This gift from above.
The words are chosen for me,
I say them as my heart can see.
How beautiful any human being can be.
Feel good and live free.

5 – The woman

Nobody knows.
She is not silent, talks a lot,
Her heart never shows.
Shares lots of smiles,
Has no regrets,
Try not to make anyone upset.
The woman
With a lovely heart
Listens to others
Offering trust.
She is not alone,
Got a family and a home.

6 – Happy Mother's Day

Mother
Is grace, love, and attention,
Care and unselfish devotion.
Mother hides her struggles while
their children make water bubbles,
Gets impressed when the child tries their best,
Smiles and plays
When her child has a great day.
Mother hides her fears,
so her child grows with no tears.
After school is done, she waits by the door,
Gives a welcome to the precious child she adores.
When child is ill, she keeps herself awake
for a hug and to give a pill.
Mother gets frustrated and many times is tired,
But looking after the child is her desire.
Mother cannot sleep
While the child weeps.
Mother doesn't rest after doing everything
without interest,
So many tasks to do,
She may not take time off because of you.
Mothers are not perfect
But deserve all the respect
For giving all they can.
Don't forget,
One day the child will be a mum,
The mother a gran.

7 – Be You

Be you,
Unique.
Don't make bad choices,
They are not a big deal.
It's ok
To feel scared,
Nobody knows tomorrow,
So, keep the good vibes instead.
Anyone can say anything,
So, listen, only to the words that sound amazing.
Give your attention
First to your heart
Then to the nation.
Love is in every human;
Create love and feel the passion.

8 – Love

Is so immense
It's profound.
Graceful for everyone to share and enjoy,
Give and receive.
For love is the most amazing feeling you will achieve.
Don't let yourself believe love is hard.
It's a gift that everyone has.
Wonderful as a beating loving heart.
Let Love be in your present
Not just in your past.
Feel loved.
It may forever last.

9 – Heaven

In heaven
Where I feel the peace and
Love,
My understanding is that heaven on earth
is the biggest gift of our Lord.
Heaven is here in my daily
Life; is the strength and the light.
It is not a dream
I see, feel, and touch.
It is not a vision'
Doesn't matter what.
Heaven is here
In my heart.

10 – Be free

Let it go.
It's so easy with words,
Emotions hide deep down.
We are surviving,
Smiling like a clown.
It is fair when you cry,
you feel alone and let the tears run by.
The face gets wet, your eyes too,
But we tend to forget the person
who loves always stands by you.
Emotions are beautiful, smiles, cries,
happiness, and much more.
Look and feel them
With an open door.
Don't hide and keep feelings faraway.
They live with you, doesn't matter what you say.
Easier said than done;
Open your heart,
You won't feel alone …

11 – The People

My eyes look.
The most amazing are the people of the world.
They have the capacity to forgive,
appreciate, give, and love,
So many things we do have,
Our souls keep us forever alive.
We try very hard
To have everything, even making us work like mad.
The people of the world are me and you;
We create happiness, wherever is possible to do.
Our hearts appreciate every kind gesture;
Loving everyone is not a simple adventure.
It's so important to pay all attention;
people in your life are like a blossom,
Needing care, understanding, and devotion.
Believe the people of our world are the greatest of
God's creations ...

12 – Love is love

When love comes
Into your life,
Creates happiness
Which makes you strive.
Let it shine
Like your first time.
Be open,
Grateful,
Compassionate.
Love comes to stay,
Enjoy this soulmate.
Here to stay
By your side,
To make you best.
Love is love
Simply does it all
Without interest.

13 – Rainy Day

On a rainy day,
Beauty comes to stay.
We all get wet
We get impress.
Free come along
Making so many things
Grow and strong.
Beauty falls on the ground,
It's like music, it has a sound.
The sky plays its part,
Listen with attention.
Rain makes us stronger as a nation.
It's true, many prefer the sky
When it's only blue.
Rain keeps you alive;
Drinking the water
Is the way to survive.

14 – Don't stop

Life is not only a wonderful journey.
It brings the worst and the best
for any human being to see.
Closing the eyes and heart
It's hard to look
When all the good things fall apart.
Do not despair.
Keep hope,
One day sun arrives,
Surprising
All the world.
Nobody knows what will come from above.
Like the sun
Shines without any set time.
Be yourself,
Try your best,
Trust someone else,
Keep going,
You will be fine.
Don't stop,
Follow your light,
Day and night.
Feel compassionate,
Be blessed,
Stay safe.

15 – Greatest feeling of all

Greatest feeling of all
Is love and gratitude.
Compassion towards yourself is needed
as much your attitude;
Easy to complain
When it's not achieved; it feels like emotional pain.
Do not regret all your mistakes.
Most of them need just a word;
There is always another direction you can take.
Many say life is hard itself,
You're never a failure when you try to do your best.
Pain is normal, like tears in the eyes,
many difficult situations, you can only say goodbye.
Keep going, use each step and
believe you can touch the universe.
You and I plus all the world are blessed
with the light of our Lord.
Create peace, create your best
Love.

16 – In our world

We are great humans,
capable of creating love for ourselves,
others, and the universe.
Unbelievable is life,
But a journey everyone needs to take.
Feel blessed, its ok to make a mistake;
Our human brain
Works to be perfect,
No need to worry
Every day is a different story.
How beautiful is our world
When we share gratitude and everything
is created by the Lord?
Feel amazing;
Imagination is there to feel
Emotions and great well-being.
Don't feel scared,
Love yourself instead

17 – Faith

God is the greatest.
Always believe
You are the only one
That things for you can be achieved.
Remember all yourself;
Keep going,
You are the only
To impress.

18 – It's Amazing

It would be amazing in our world,
If nobody would be starving.
Food, education, love, and care would be everywhere.
If the war ended, not any country
or person would be offended.
It would be amazing if no more competitions
between the nations.
All living free under the same fruity tree.
It would be wonderful showing respect
and compassion to each other.
Living together like the best sister or brother.

19 – Rainbow

Brings colours to the cloudy sky.
A light drizzle may fall,
But I will stand by.
I won't despair if sun says goodbye.
Blue skies will bring
Hope and grace.
I will carry on,
Doesn't matter how long it takes

20 – Christmas Day

Family celebrations,
Son of God has born.
Early mass sharing smiles and hugs.
Having someone to visit,
Present Christmas list.
I am not alone,
Christmas has brought love to my home.

21 – The light

Is intense and bright.
Creating hope and love
In my heart, in my world.
Thank you for being the
Light in my life
My Lord.

22 – No words

To describe the gratitude
Of our wonderful human side.
It is all good,
Creates the most amazing vibe.
Don't think and regret
for every lesson in life teaches you to show respect.

23 – The days

Where we are pain free.
They are so beautiful as they can be.
How much we want to enjoy a day of happiness.
Too many things,
I guess perhaps no words needed.
Just a beautiful thought and
Inner happiness can be achieved.
Think what feels the best;
Feel in peace,
Love, and rest.

24 – Strength

Drives you to believe
What is done with a good heart
It's always possible to achieve.
It's not only one direction,
You need strength in any difficult situation.
Keep your eyes in your heart;
Strength grows from your present
and also from your past.
Keep strong,
No worries,
Strength will guide you
With a little touch.

25 – Good choice

Let yourself
Grow with love and grace,
Feel loved,
So many things are hard to embrace.
Be strong, carry on,
it doesn't matter how long it takes.
The journey of life is the most amazing,
it can surprise you with the smallest thing.

26 – Moving house

The house,
Is empty.
In silence, no sound
Above the floor, even on the ground.
The walls all plain,
Not hanging pictures,
Or any toys.
Remember you looking after the girls and boys.
Loud noises, little angel voices
Are not heard anymore;
Even the bell
Has stopped,
Nobody at your door.
I got shivers,
The emptiness
I will remember
Of friendship and happiness.

27 – Warmth

Is close to your heart,
Gives comfort any time
Need to feel it
Just touch.
Not a surprise warmth,
Bring you love
Into the present
Not in the past.
Let it stay,
May it forever last.

28 – The sun

Brings light
To earth and our life.
Where are you?
Feeling sad when everything is here for you.
Nothing is done
Without grace.
Feel loved,
And yourself
Embrace.

29 – Relax

Breath
The deep breath
We all need to take
In hard times is never fake.
Giving a voice to our inner side,
It's not an easier ride.
Our feelings of love, gratitude, compassion, and pain.
Feeling alone when saine.
The deep breath
Is here to help,
Just close your eyes,
and peacefully rest.

30 – Discover

Discover
a wonderful treasure
With a beautiful soul,
a beautiful heart
Shinning everyday
In the dark or brighter day.
Big or small,
Its light
Illuminates the road.
Take it in,
Nothing is done without attitude.
The light you need to take care.
Be blessed,
From everywhere,
Then discover, it's all about you.
The choices you can make
What matters to you
Remember the light
It's always you.

31 – May the Queen rest in peace

The Queen,
Passed away,
Without being aware she can bring
the sense of loss,
Everyday.
It's sad I say
In our world of choice
We cannot choose to stay.
Life is the journey of the living,
With an end and a beginning.
We all leave family and friends behind,
Even the Queen,
Her rein by God,
Had to resign.
No choice to come to the world and leave.
It's all in the hands of God
I believe.
Carry on with our lives,
And accept we all one day have to die.
Life is beautiful,
It's a learning path.
Remember to live for your present
Not for your past.
Live life,
May it long last.

32 – Love

Loves you;
Love is the greatest creation.
Love grows everyday
Like a flower,
You need to water it anyway.
It surprises me how many want love,
But just sit and wait,
For it to be sent by God.
If you believe in love,
You need to find it, look at it, and most, appreciate it.
All love is good, no need to argue and negotiate.
Love is free, creative,
Love is for everyone from the most
intelligent to the naive.
Love doesn't choose you,
You are the one
To make the choice,
To love or to rejoice.
Love comes and goes,
Never for good.
Love loves you
Whether you are in a good or bad mood.
Love is love,
Simple,
Live with a smile, let love
Take care of you
For a while.

33 – Faith

Faith
Is the hope
You need every day.
It keeps your dreams alive in anyway.
Keep your good heart
Thoughts, and believe,
With good intentions,
Anything you can achieve.
Don't ever show sadness,
When things get out of interest.
Life is only a journey;
The one,
We must never,
Regret.

34 – The gift of life

The gift of life,
Is to love.
Appreciate all given from above.
The sky can be blue, but if you don't admire it,
it won't mean anything to you.
The clouds can be in many different colours,
But when dark, they give water to our flowers.
The sea can be so blue.
Be yourself, nobody in the world is like you.
The earth and universe
Just accept the freedom, peace, and love,
Gifts for you sent
By the Lord

35 – Angels in the world

There are angels
In this world.
The ones who share
Compassion, care, and love.
It's true,
The angels in the world
want the best for you.
Bring all the joy,
To your inner self.
Stay peaceful,
Feel blessed.
Unique is the word;
Nobody is like yourself.

36 – Feelings

I have met feelings of joy and sadness.
The ones my eyes can show
When I cry or glow.
The tear drops, feelings of hope.
The bad days already gone,
I found a place like home.
Feelings about the world I see.
Nature, sky, and sea.
How beautiful feelings can be.
Choose them in your imagination,
love should be every human creation.
Feelings should not make you upset,
it's all part of a life process.
Feelings with no regret.
You are wonderful.
Only tried your best.

37 – Love, Gratitude, and Kindness

Time goes
when feeling loved
By nature, by God.
It's all so beautiful when our
hearts are happy souls.
Keep believing it's free
Which direction you take.
Be real to yourself; so many beautiful
diamonds shine but are fake.
True beauty grows slowly
By the action, believes and words we say.
Sometimes it's all we need to create our happiness.
So many things depend on us.
We tend to forget all we need is to share love,
gratitude, and kindness.

38 – Let it go.

It's so easy with words
Emotions hide deep down
We survive them,
Smiling like a clown.
It is fair when you cry, you feel alone
and let the tears run by.
The face gets wet, your eyes too.
But we tend to forget the person
who loves will always stand by you.
Emotions are beautiful, smiles,
tears of happiness and much more.
Look and feel them
With an open door.
Don't hide and keep them faraway.
They live within you, doesn't matter what you say.
Easier said than done.
Open your heart,
You won't feel alone.

39 – Trust

Is everything I need from you.
Keep my words, smiles, tears,
and everything else you know is true.
Simple,
Life without trust,
How hard it can be.
It's not about only the feelings,
the thoughts, and the heart.
Day by day,
The best is to have someone
We can Trust.
In our lives, right now,
the future, and the past.

40 – Flowers

One of the greatest gifts of nature.
Growing on the ground,
Sharing the perfume,
Dancing together.
I assume
Our hearts feel loved
By receiving flowers;
We feel the blessing from God.
Admire this gesture,
Receiving the flowers with great pleasure.
Isn't that true?
The flowers bring the best in our heart.
They are love,
Showing care
With a simple touch.
Look around,
You too are a beautiful flower.
Feel free, doesn't matter if under the tree
Received all the good
Like a flower, feel loved, appreciated, and above all,
Feel gratitude

41 – What is love?

Love is a creation,
By a human being.
We share our emotion.
Love is simple,
Can be everywhere, don't miss it,
Be aware.
Love grows,
Like the wind when it blows.
It is spread with strength and kindness.
Love is above all the greatest.
Vision of happiness,
Stay with you
If given a space to live, appreciate
and feel blessed ...

42 – I'm light

In my heart,
When I love myself,
Leave other things apart.
The beauty inside of my mind, heart, and body.
This light I feel is given to me by God.
I'm the light,
In my world.
Bring peace,
Gratitude,
Faith,
Hope, and all good from above.

43 – Hard times

Feel,
When times are hard,
You feel alone.
Like in the dark,
Sadness is part of your heart.
The dark days
May take time to pass.
Remember like a flower,
Nothing grows too fast,
It's life,
You have only to adjust.
No pain,
No rain,
No snow or tears are here to ever last.
Believe the struggles will become
Things of the past.
Nothing lasts,
Apart from love,
All good things from above.

44 – The child

Who holds mum's hand,
Feels her heart beating.
Hopes the mother will not be leaving.
They will stay together.
Dreading the separation and losing the mum forever,
The anxiety that it can be real,
For the child it's a big deal.
How to survive without mum's love.
Only hope mum will take care of the child from above.
The blue sky, sun, and stars
Will remind the child that
Mum is not far.

45 – The night

Is so beautiful and quiet.
You rest in the dark,
Separate from daylight.
The thoughts and imagination can be stronger.
Sleeping sometimes is not right.
But who can blame the night?
It's the same for everyone,
Dark with lots of stars to shine.
Peaceful it can be.
It's why in the dark we cannot see.
To be honest,
I love the night when my sleep is the best.

46 – Feelings

My heart is my soul,
Feeling the love.
I'm beautiful,
As the blue sky above
Where the stars
Later will shine.
I will be one of them
When resting my mind.
My eyes will be closed,
But I'll be fine.
The dreams will become reality.
I won't compare
In my dream,
Life is amazingly fair.

47 – The words

We wait to hear,
Sound like,
Are you OK my dear?
The silences in our hearts
Are so deep,
Nobody listens,
We weep.
Despair is not there.
A room without light,
Alone.
Nobody to touch.
I want you to know,
Silence for years
Is giving a sad feeling somehow.
The words of love, kindness, compassion
Used to bring to my life passion.
Not hearing these words anymore.
Nobody comes to see me,
Or knocks on my door.
I'm home,
But it's the outside
I adore.

48 – Friendship lasts forever

My friend,
Missing you very much.
So far in heaven but still in my heart.
The school days, laughs, care,
and protection are far away.
I thank you for my best days,
Where I was afraid that others will hurt me,
You were there to comfort and hold me.
I still remember we were angels full of joy,
Where our happiness
Others felt they could destroy.
We had plans,
To study and have lots of fun.
The time came,
where so young, you left this world.
Still believe you're my best friend,
In my heart, from above.
From the sky,
Walk with me in this world.
I will never
Say goodbye.

49 – Family

The treasure of your life.
They give you what they can,
Always staying by your side.
Keep the family
You love strong.
Whenever lost,
You will feel where you belong.
The affection, respect,
It will be there,
You won't be lost.
Find your home,
It's always been there.
If you ever despair,
Family
Is the tree
With lots of branches
Where you grow free,
The roots firm on the ground
It's listening to your sound.
Don't feel upset, sometimes even family forget.
The most precious gift
Is a happy family
Where peace and love exist.
Family
Can bring lots of happiness.
Don't waste your time
With material things to feel impressed.
Good heart,
Compassion, understanding are always the best.

50 – New days

Enthusiasm
To start is the best way.
Give yourself a big lovely
Hug.
Bring love,
Smiles, and hope.
It's a new start of light.
Be the sun,
Be the light.

51 – The time goes

All good memories are kept.
I look up to the sky,
Feeling you nearby.
Smiling, I say hello,
You're watching me all this time.
I hold your hand and you hold mine.
I shed a tear,
Hearing your voice,
You will be ok, my dear.
Always wishing the best for you.
Our friendship is forever true.

52 – No words

Say what your heart feels,
It helps and heals.
The suffering and pain
We all carry in vain.
Say deserve respect
As I try all my best.
Don't worry about your tears,
They bring out your fears.

53 – New day

Wake up
I'm here,
Taking a deep breath,
Feeling strong where I belong.
I will be walking around
Looking all the earth and roots of the tree
Firm on the ground.

54 – Pain

Pain is difficult to take in,
Pain is the world sometimes you live in,
But the pain will one day end.
You will have something great, new and not pretend.
The compassion for you is something that will be new.
You need to care of yourself.
When perhaps there is nobody else,
You will dream to love your heart and life,
Then you realise life is not fair.
Don't forget the past,
Seek and remember.
It may be useful to remember that moment
when you felt love and everything there to last.
The love you received,
The attention you gave,
The smiles you shared,
The wonderful emotions you have brought;
remember, they all there for you.
Carry on believing that someone else out there cares
And is with you when disperse.
Be kind to yourself;
It's hard to accept that life sometimes is unfair.
You need to shine and know that I was
with you in that light.
Believe in yourself and carry on,
Believe you're smart.

55 – Dreams

It'll be amazing,
If in our world,
Nobody will be starving.
Love and care
Would be everywhere.
The war will have an end,
No country or person would be offended.
Amazing would be we could live together
like all the trees.
It would be amazing
If you share the good to each other
Like the best sister or brother.
It would be amazing
If having not to pretend
That happiness never ends.

56 – Spring

Bright and sunny day,
Not too hot I may say.
Blossom everywhere,
The white flower of the cherry tree,
Underneath, yellow is all I see.
Head out of the window looking around.
Amazed how beautiful is the ground.
I will never forget
The amazing nature
Have met.

Spring to be kept with love and colour.
The perfume of every flower.
The small touch of love,
Given by nature,
Created by the Lord.
Small birds hanging in small branches
Singing their own songs
Like an orchestra
Deep and clear
For everyone to hear.

Gentle breeze
Blows slowly on my face and hair
Feeling looked after
By nature with its care.
Suddenly, the silence arrives,
Birds have paused.
Human voices
Coming along
To smell the perfume
Of the roses.

I am here,
This is my world
Nothing to worry
For moment a kept
My eyes closed.

57 – Missing you

Is my feeling today.
I want you to know,
I care, I'm far away.
Your blessings,
Smiles, and kindness,
The moments we have shared are in my heart.
When feeling alone,
I bring compassion to myself
And say,
I feel you,
I'm home.

58 – Care

You are the one
Take care of yourself.
It's sad but true.
Be the one responsible for you.
Show the most important goodness.
Give yourself
Simply the best.
Care, compassion, and love.
Everything is here for you.
Feel blessed from
The above.

59 – My body

Magic; my heart beats,
It races when we are happy at least.
The magic of human lives,
Smile, touch, feel, understand, and vibe.
Efforts small or big,
Like the ground we dig.
Hands gently care, touch, and share.
Smiles not just showing our teeth,
but to show happiness and other things to delete.
Eyes to see
Our world including you and me.
Head works hard,
Making us work in the good and bad.
Brain challenges our thoughts, right or wrong;
so many decisions in our head belong.
Legs keep us moving all the way.
On the good on bad days.
Our body
Carries all we have,
Without a question
It is fab.
The magician I can see,
Is the life my body offers to me.
Pain free.
Body is the greatest when it does its best.
Magic happens every day.
Be the magician and take good care of you anyway.

60 – Colour

Dark or light,
Stars shining through the night.
It's time to sleep,
Looking at the sky, emotions are clear or deep.
I am small,
Standing high,
I don't fall.
Always up there,
Looking down,
I can see everywhere.
Magic heaven
I salute, peace is here,
Don't need to worry anymore.
I just have you at night,
When walk out of the door.
Give me the calm I need,
In you I see all beautiful indeed.
My heart feels intense,
May need to cry,
Say any word.
Night you are here,
My soul,
My world.

61 – Hope

Is not only a word.
Is a belief in yourself and GOD,
Strength when feeling alone,
Lost in your own home.
Hope is faith,
God is the light
Guiding you through the night.
Hope never gives up,
Here to last,
Patience,
Don't stop,
Keep believing,
Keep hope.

62 – Be you

Beautiful,
Play for your soul
Music by heart.
See yourself the centre of the universe,
Like you nobody else
Wise and compassionate.
Love you,
Own soulmate,
Find happiness.
Life is a gift,
The greatest of all,
Stay strong,
Even if you fall.

63 – The angel

Who came to me
I was alone
Away from home;
I felt despair nobody cares.
The angel
Looked in my eyes;
I was sad,
I had to say so many goodbyes.
The tears were in the heart,
Smiles hid with fear.
Words I wanted to share,
But who was there.
The angel
Calmly hugged me,
Gave me strength,
Offered me a smile,
Held my hand.
I felt happy for a while.
The angel offers compassion,
Stays with me
When I need
Love and attention

64 – Attitude

Many words
Never being heard
The great human beings
Do all good,
Achieve anything instead
We must not forget
The good we do,
Never regret.
It's true,
You don't need to impress,
The good stays with you.
Feel good,
You are the best.

65 – Garden

In a beautiful green garden
Many are like me
Sharing the same world,
Picked by a loving heart,
Kindness for someone just passed.
Lucky you to be carried
Looked after, loved, appreciated,
The beauty of the perfume,
Colours of leaves,
Art of the flower,
Everything you have and you can see.
The flowers left in the garden
Are like you me.
All happy to be taken to success,
I stayed behind.
But I am still
In the garden of the best.

66 – The human

The heart, body, and mind;
Everything is needed to keep me alive.
I need not just water, oxygen, and blood,
without care and love I won't survive.
It is funny, even a baby needs a dummy;
I need attention, praise, friendship, hugs, and
compassion.
My world is not only a human creation,
is universe, God at his best.
I can see the sky,
The little stars in the dark.
We humans are strong
To keep all people of the world
Together in one only
Big heart where everyone
Belongs.

67 – Feel

When times are hard
You feel alone, like in the dark,
Sadness is part of your heart.
The dark days may take time to pass,
Remember, like a flower, nothing grows fast,
It's life, you only have to adjust,
No pain, rain, snow, or tears are ever to last.
Believe the struggles will become things of the past.
Nothing lasts, only love, all the good things
From above.

68 – The peoples of the world

Have red flowers for love,
White for peace,
Black for night,
Blue for sky and sea.
We are all humans, colours first thing we see.
We are colourful.
Say no to racism and spray the word
We are human, must not forget
That our colours are nothing to regret

69 – Why say

I am black or white,
Equality should be our biggest right.
Look at a kind human heart.
We are all beautiful
No doubt.
All people of the world,
You are loved
By nature, and the Lord.

70 – The Child

Watches, feels stood by.
It's a bad world
When many women feel powerless and cry.
Who is there?
The child the only one who cares.
It's the child's world,
Feels parallelised, cannot express any word.
The pain is around,
Feel it from shaking underground.
The screams, the only voice
Begging to live,
Being alone at home.
Nobody came
Until this day,
The child has the memories,
They are never far away.

71 – Love

Is not hidden
Under the ground
It's all around.
Don't say you can't see
Love when birds sing above that tree.
When the rain plays its own sound,
The wind spreads all the leaves around.
Where little flowers smile to you
and the sky is dark and blue.
Love is deep,
Always in your heart.
Let it grow,
Give it a hug.
Love is Love,
Don't keep it close in your bag.

EIN HERZ FÜR AUTOREN A HEART FOR AUTHORS À L'ÉCOUTE DES AUTEURS MIA KAP
HJÄRTA FÖR FÖRFATTARE UN CORAZÓN POR LOS AUTORES YAZARLARIMIZA GÖNÜL
CUORE PER AUTORI ET HJERTE FOR FORFATTERE EEN HART VOOR SCHRIJVERS TEN
HERZÖINKÉRT SERCE DLA AUTORÓW EIN HERZ FÜR AUTOREN A HEART FOR AUTHC
MIGRAÇÃO ВСЕЙ ДУШОЙ К АВТОРАМ ETT HJÄRTA FÖR FÖRFATTARE À LA ESCUCHA D
AUTEURS MIA ΚΑΡΔΙΑ ΓΙΑ ΣΥΓΓΡΑΦΕΙΣ UN CUORE PER AUTORI ET HJERTE FOR FORFA
YAZARLARIMIZA GÖNÜL VERS HERZÖINKÉRT SERCE DLA AUTORÓW I
VOOR SCHRIJVERS TEN ONS RAÇÃO ВСЕЙ ДУШОЙ К АВТОРАМ ETT

The author

Goreti was born in Madeira, Portugal, in 1972 to a large family. She lived in the countryside in a small house with her parents and siblings. Her parents worked on the farm all their lives. One of the youngest, Goreti left secondary school to help with jobs at home and on the farm. She spent her adolescence working hard.

Goreti's diaries were her best friend where she could express all her worries and fears with a belief her life would always have a positive outcome. She had lots of imaginative thoughts and her dream was to live in a better world.
Due to a lack of opportunities for work in Madeira, Goreti emigrated to London in 1996 to learn English as a foreign language. Her intention was to return to Madeira and work in the tourism industry, but she ended up staying in England. During COVID-19, to pass her free time, she started to write poems in English. Goreti has lived in London for almost 20 years. She is married and has two children.